White Hibiscus

Loribelle Spirovski

Loribelle Spirovski attended the College of Fine Arts at the University of NSW and has worked as a visual artist since 2014. She paints out of a boundless curiosity for the human condition, reconceptualising images from her immediate world and online, to parse the unique anxieties of the early 21st century. Working across diverse styles, Loribelle reflects on her own rich history and the connective tissue between tradition and innovation. After a celebrated artistic career she now turns to writing after a long period as a dedicated reader. She lives in Sydney with her husband and cat. *White Hibiscus* is her first book. www.loribellespirovski.com

Loribelle Spirovski

White Hibiscus

UPSWELL

First published in Australia in 2025
by Upswell Publishing
Perth, Western Australia
upswellpublishing.com

Upswell operates in the city of Perth, on ancient country of the Whadjuk people of the Noongar nation who remain the spiritual and cultural custodians of this beautiful land. We acknowledge their continuing connection to country and express gratitude to elders past and present for their strength and creativity … Always was, always will be, Aboriginal land.

This is a work of fiction and does not represent individuals, living or from the past, in its pages.

ISBN: 978-0-645-98405-7

A catalogue record for this book is available from the National Library of Australia

Cover design by Chil3, Fremantle
Typeset in Foundry Origin by Lasertype
Printed by McPherson's Printing Group

Upswell Publishing is assisted by the State of Western Australia through its funding program for arts and culture.

For

Belinda, Simon and Lobel

Now I see; I remember better what I felt the other day on the seashore when I was holding that pebble. It was a sort of sweet disgust. How unpleasant it was! And it came from the pebble, I'm sure of that, it passed from the pebble into my hands...a sort of nausea...

Jean-Paul Sartre, Nausea

My eyes are wild; my lips tightly pressed.
The bird flies: the flower dances;
but I hear always the sullen thud of the waves;
and the chained beast stamps on the beach.
It stamps and stamps.

Virginia Woolf, The Waves

When touched the plant closes in on itself like a small palm.

Run a finger down the dividing vein and its fronds collapse from the point of contact. A dance of a thousand hands in miniature.

Although possessing a Tagalog name, the introduced species originates from South and Central America.

Known colloquially as 'Makahiya', which means shy, it is also sometimes 'Shameplant' and 'Touch-me-not' and is ubiquitous in the Philippines.

In the last decade biologists have studied the plant's ability to seemingly remember past encounters, learning the kinds of touch that are non-threatening and the ones that are dangerous.

PART 1

one

blue
white
red

navy eggshell burgundy

the blue of the ocean (which isn't always blue)

the colour of his skin

the colour of blood

On other walls

portholes like ellipses
broke the illusion
of being inside a hotel.

Everywhere else
wallpaper alternated
in shades of the three colours.

Ceilings curved with
panels of polished wood
every wall ornamented

with a screen or painting
or unmovable light fixture
glowing sun-coloured light

no visible part of the ship was left unadorned.

And because it was a ship
commonplace things were
new and interesting again
like when we were children.

> –"This must be the bar."
> –"This must be the casino."
> –"This must be where you go to eat."

Wherever wood or tile
gave way to carpet
footsteps became inaudible
as though you disappeared
every now and then and
rematerialised across the room.

Nearly all the guests were American.

In the Atrium
screens advertised
Pilates on Tuesdays
bridge classes the morning after
courses on Word and
Excel the following week etc.

One slide showed
an honour roll of names:
Phillis O–, Sally-Anne B– and Linda P–
held diamond memberships.

Nora S– and Margaret T–
have sailed on this ship
every year since 2001.

Betty M– was a permanent resident.

And then his face
appeared on a screen

he tenses

(self-conscious)
(a gentle thrill?)

In the picture
he's dressed in a tuxedo
next to the partial silhouette
of a piano.

A Gatsby-style backdrop
Photoshopped behind him.

–God I look young.
–When was that taken?
–About ten years ago, I think.
–Wow. I wasn't even born yet.

laughs *laughs*

He sipped his coffee
which tasted only mildly
of detergent

and then one of the passengers
noticing the poster for his concert
caught his eye
and began to approach

—Let's go somewhere quieter.
—Ok.

We walked up
to the highest deck
exiting at the sign
of an arrow pointing left.

—What's the arrow for?
—I think it's so people don't walk into each other.

—But don't people know how to do that?

We walked past the tennis court,
golf course, and through a pair
of glass doors that opened to the pool
where sunbathers dressed
in tropical bird colours
shaded their faces behind
the shadows of raised books.

Husbands lay deflated
on reclining chairs.

Across the deck the pool
was a hand mirror to the sky.

We walked to the shade
waiting for our eyes
to adjust to the dark
and found a foyer opening up
to a large room.

Palm Court in gilt letters
next to the hand-sanitising station

It was a large fan-shaped room
full of skylights that threw down
sun in slanting rays.

Palm trees swelled
from porcelain vases
large enough to hide a man.

Frond tips so tall
they touched the ceiling
like a Palm Sunday march.

Instead of walls
wide windows wrapped
the room in a pink-tinted glow
that made the sky look always
on the verge of sunset.

It was empty around noon
when most passengers were
swimming, gambling, shopping
and waiters appeared hoisting
silver trays like birdcages.

Each crew member had a name badge
identifying their country of origin
so we were waited on by both
Mark Canada and Mark Philippines.

        From what I could tell
at least seventy percent
of the crew were Filipino.

Something that surprised me
until a Google search confirmed
that this was apparently a thing
on cruise ships.

> "I've sailed for more than 30 years and Filipinos are the most hard-working people. Others need to be prodded into doing work or else demand more wages for less work.
>
> Filipino agencies have a strict discipline board, so even the slightest transgression can result in the loss of a well-paying job. I would choose a Filipino seaman any day."
>
> —Quora.com

Each Filipino crew member
seemed familiar to me.

Like a person I'd met before
whose features had shifted
just enough to be
someone else.

They were all men
so in each face I'd see
a cousin or an uncle.

Except for room attendants
and the lounge singer. (aunts)

When the first crew member
recognised me as one of his kind
we exchanged knowing smiles

speaking in a grey language
of broken words and
embarrassed laughter
that (I hoped) hid evidence
of my forgotten tongue.

While walking
down Manila streets
I remember people
teasing my mother
about where she'd found
the white child whose
sweaty hand she held
as though I was only a flower
she'd plucked by the roadside.

I didn't look particularly Filipino.

I'd search my reflection
for signs that gave me away.

Watch the features shift
from my mother's to my
father's and back again.

But Filipinos always knew.
In the way family knew.

And it wasn't really anything
the crew could see.

I always sought their eye first.

A wordless invitation.

They would look—really look
and they would ask

and then I would feel

as though I belonged.

two

my mother pregnant (Pasay city)

Vita (sister) and Efren (her husband) invite her to stay (spare room)

she spends afternoons
at *manay* Gloria's shop
grazing on *bangus*
freshly picked papaya
plucking *tinapa* flesh
drinking the water of coconuts
eating salted slices
of sour mangoes
shaped like a human heart
resting by the shade
of a *Bani* tree
humming to herself
(to us)

a breeze dances
at the hem of her dress
smoke rising
from idling *jipneys*
and their stunted *traysikel* brothers

she turns
so she can't see them

(later, she tells me
that she only wanted
to look at beautiful things

so that her child
would be beautiful)

and like this
we celebrate her first
and only birthday (30)
in the same body

then

blood

the shade of raspberry jam
on her underwear

Efren escorts her to the hospital

I imagine her
describing it all to me
what was happening
where we were going
reassuring (herself) me

her voice
through membrane
and amniotic fluid
into my bones
coming from inside

and outside of me
so that it must
have felt like God

a ward of five

one of two
first-time mothers

the experienced ones
share their stories
sparkling eyes, skin golden,
slick, soft with sweat
fanning themselves
with fax-paper folded
into Japanese fans
our labour lasts five hours

when the obstetrician pulls me out
my mother is alone we are alone

and she holds me to her chest

and sings to me
(to us)

three

"We would always sit in Magdalena's section every morning. She is so joyful and full of energy."

—bworldonline.com

After breakfast
the usual tempo of the ship
leisurely and dreamlike
took on the pace and organisation
of an enormous ant farm

Passengers in collapsible hats
and Birkenstocks formed lines
towards reception, picked up their
passports, filed down to level four
collected permits and swipe cards
and exited by the metal detectors
onto small boats that carried them
the short distance to shore

Outside, Noumea

a tree-lined peninsula
gliding beyond portholes
like a zoetrope

While passengers disembarked
'What a Wonderful World'
played so loudly
over the speakers
that you could do
nothing but sit
and wait for it to finish

I see trees of green
red roses too
I see them bloom
for me and you

We walked to reception
picked up our passports
filed down to level four
collected permits and swipe
cards exited by the metal detectors
onto a small boat that carried us
the short distance to shore

on Noumea we walked

not to any particular place

more to remember
what walking on earth felt like
as he described what he remembered
of the city from when he toured there
with a youth orchestra in his early teens

Most things were different

On the beach
Kanak children
darted in and out of waves

pearls of seafoam
adorning their brown skin
curling in golden hair

I sketched them
with fingers
greasy with chip-oil
burrowing my toes
in the white sand

dark eyes large in their faces
sunkissed hair frizzing
into gold-tipped threads
t-shirts and shorts
heavy with seawater

the littlest
naked except for a pair
of gold earrings
rolled in the sand
emerging sugar-coated

there's a yellow submarine
on the eldest's shirt
and underneath it:
the words *le grand bleu*

he called out in French
rounding them up
half-heartedly
the two still in the water
launching into somersaults
determined to make the most
of their last few minutes

the briefest and sweetest

then the little one
turned

and looked my way

and I reappeared from
the non-place I'd
been watching from

and I sensed it
before I saw it

an animal's corpse splayed
on the edge of the sidewalk

its body was hollow with death
its insides swarming with so many
flies that for a moment I couldn't
understand what I was seeing

a petrol-coloured thing
eddying purling in endless swells
of order of chaos of endless
trembling trembling trembling

somewhere in the distance

the sound of construction work

a leviathan

four

when they'd been young/alive
my grandparents ran
a small general store
at the front of their house
at the foot of a hill
beneath the school
where the children went

my grandfather
taught his nine children
to count money
twist *polvoron* into
candy-coloured cellophane
bag peanut brittle

his palms smooth
with coconut oil
though no less durable
when dispensing
order among his
children (wife)

in between shifts
the children
would run barefoot
among banana trees
and *abaca* fibres
like strands of flaxen hair
kicking fallen banana hearts
until the purple petals splayed

until *tatay*
extracted
the rattan stick
he kept for such
threats

Ah!
how my *lolo*
loved to play music
and make
the children sing
to neighbours
who came
like fireflies
in the dry season

mosquito
coils
scent
the memories

frying
fish
fumes

jipney
smut

acetone
cuticles

of *titas*
in plastic
tsinelas

talcum
powder
on children's
skin
hiding *libag*
under
fleshy
necks

the verdant
odour
of *gumamela*
petals
red as a
woman's
mouth

the tail end
of wet season

I am a fold
in the crook
of my mother's arm

and my uncle's final
vibrating note wilts
in the humid air

as he passes
the microphone to her
like a relay baton

—she'd sing like this
microphone in one hand
me in the other

the tremor of her
blossoming
into my ribcage

as neighbours watched
with eyes that combed
her skin

I'd feel their gaze
on her (on me)
as though we still
shared the same body
and cry

she'd move us then
to a quiet room

away from the rest

safe

five

"Your room's attendant is called **Maria**
and she is happy to serve you."

When ***Maria*** finished
making up the room
the sheets were tucked
so tightly that from the
doorway the bed looked
like a gallery plinth.

I imagined what ***Maria***
had thought of the small
brown stain on the linen
(from coffee spilled earlier)

If she'd wondered about it
(food? shit? blood?)
whether she'd painted a
(lazy? gross? uncivilised?)
picture of us in her mind.

I sat on the edge
not wanting to spoil
her perfect work
bowing down to the
leather straps on
my heeled sandals.

Even when the ship was busy
it was never crowded.

The passengers, mostly old
some elderly, reluctant to be
in too close a proximity
to others—always kept
a polite distance.

I noticed that if they sensed
a crowd forming
they instinctively stepped back
waiting for numbers to disperse

—That's how you can tell if the clientele is a luxury one.

When we arrived at The Dining Room
not so much a crowd, but a sensible queue
stretched past the concierge desk.

Prada bag
Ralph Lauren sweater
Chanel espadrilles
Saint Laurent bag
Gucci shirt
Chanel espadrilles

Before we got on the ship
he told me that as we weren't
actually paying guests
we were expected to let
other passengers go before us
if we were ever in a queue

as a courtesy.

So when we reached the front
ten minutes later
the maître d gave us
a telepathic look
and we stepped aside
allowing an elderly couple
to enter the hall before us.

When our turn came
we were led by a young
good-looking waiter (they were all young and good looking)
past the tables
by the window
with a view of the ocean
to one closer
to the room's centre
with a view of the
tables by the window.

Then waiters ushered
another pair of guests
and then another
to a table
to a table
to a table.

None of this was new to him.

The passengers on the ship
were the kind of people
who'd attended his concerts
since he was a boy.

So in each he'd see
someone familiar.

Someone he'd met before
whose features had shifted
just enough
to be someone else.

We watched them for a while
until boredom made our eyes
drift to the window

and the ebbing sea

its surface a pane of dull dimpled glass.

It was my thirtieth birthday.

> "Shout out to Fernando (Club USA, Hasting's and the Lido breakfast buffet) who always found us the best seats in the house."
>
> —cruisecritic.com

six

it was rare for me
to see my mother alone

so when I found her that day
in the kitchen of the third house

with her arms inside a metal basin
she caught me watching

and lifted her hands

> *'Dinuguan' uses the parts of the animal (pig)*
> *that are usually thrown away.*
>
> *Its name comes from the word 'dugo',*
> *meaning blood.*

and her hands were dripping
in that violent red

colour so animated
it almost leapt
on me

but there was no pain
in her face

only a funny smile
as she described

how to separate
liquid from solid

and when she placed her hands in the basin
she squeezed the crimson jelly with satisfaction

almost pleasure

there's a photo of me
inside that basin:

a foot of water
puddled at my feet
the green hose coiled
around my body
the smirk
of my vulva
peering under
tendrils
of wet hair

she told me it was around this age
that I'd vomit most of my food

unless she fed me with her bare hand
folded into a pout (the traditional way)

so she took me to the *Manghihilot*
in the village where she was born

his *nipa* hut smallest in the row
insides glowing with kerosene lamps

the *Manghihilot* rested his thin brown arms
next to banana leaves stacked like wads of cash

'Manghihilot' doesn't exactly mean 'healer'
it means 'sniffer': one who sniffs out the bad

my mother sat opposite him on the bamboo
platform that would later serve as his bed

his low raspy *Bicol* so soft I could barely hear
the words he spoke as he smeared each leaf

placed them on my back, telling me
I'd caught *something* he couldn't name

a thing that chafed against food
against air against emotions

to my mother he gave a hot drink
made from the petals of *gumamela* flowers

for the hypertension
inherited with my birth

when he finished, the *Manghihilot* folded
our money lengthwise pleated between his fingers

edging his knuckles with strange paper claws
that made currency harder to steal

outside, his elderly mother sat on the ladder-steps
playing *sunka* chewing the betel leaf vigorously

smiling with her few teeth
a fresh shade of molten red

at the time I told my mother
I didn't like the taste of spoons

too much
like the flavour of blood

but in truth

my stomach
was already full

of what I would
later recognise

as dread

seven

crumbly morsels
of black pudding
paired with
sea scallops
perfectly seared
so the crisp edges
whetted the eye
before touching
the tongue
the taste
of the sea
still abundant
in tender
white flesh

potato soup
finely pureed
velvet sweet
balanced with
fragrant leek
melts like butter
in the mouth

ragu alla Genovese
beef cheek
so tender
it yielded
to the lightest
touch of the fork
melting into ribbons
of delicate flavour

enveloped
in the subtle
textures
of candele
mother of all pasta

duck confit
burnished gold
fat crackling
under semi-
translucent skin
crisp as an autumn leaf
infused with
tender cloves
of garlic roasted
until jewel-like

layers of
mille-feuille
so fine
they made a sound
like static electricity
buds of cream
melting
into raspberries
like edible gems

on other days:
fresh tuna sashimi
like a sweet tongue
against your tongue
carpaccio so finely sliced
you could see through it
prime belly of salmon
from the Norwegian coast

garlanded with
fresh green florets
crisp as spring
cakes of every description
ruby strawberries and
pineapple, tart as gossip
rows of melon
like a traffic light
mangoes the shape
of a human heart
baked goods
deli meats
a dozen varieties
of cheese and
oysters
oysters
oysters

we ate well

eight

The colours of the rainbow
so pretty in the sky
are also on the faces
of people going by

When we reached Lautoka
I was too sick to leave the cabin

The pills I'd been taking for nausea
now gave way to fatigue
my irises like drops of ink bleeding
out into greyish pink corneas.

But the nausea brought with it a kind
of clarity—an errant cousin of peace.

I turned to him
lying next to me
tracing the topography
of pillow marks
on his skin.

He'd been to Lautoka before
so didn't mind staying on board.
(Preferred it, really.)

Through the curtain
the wharf was close enough
to see passengers carrying
handheld electric fans

as they were escorted
past shipping containers to
taxis and tricycles idling
in rows next to squinting locals.

I tried lying on my back
studying the frosted glass
on the light fixture
a finger absently circling
the birthmark on my shoulder;
a twin of one on my mother's shoulder.

My finger rested
on the small plateau of skin
pretending that our marks
were quantumly entangled
so she might feel my hand
on her shoulder.

On the wharf
a black bin liner fluttered
like a crow.

—Alright, I'm off to the gym.

and he rose from the bed
naked
pale skin luminous.

I watched him rummage for clothes.

—I think we've lost one of the key cards.

The only card left
was in the slot
that powered the room
like an old coin-operated generator.

—It's ok, I don't need light.

And when he pulled the card out
the room got slightly darker

as though to show that with his leaving
some of the light is taken from me.

door clicks shut

alone now

I could sing out loud

I do (never in front of him)

I read aloud from my book
and flip through the drawings
I'd done on the ship:

    why had I chosen to draw that?
    what had I been doing that day?

A few years ago
when he tried meditation
he was given a word in
Sanskrit to meditate on

He didn't know what
the word meant.

That helped, I think.

There'd been a private
ceremony between him
and his teacher who had
herself meditated on the word
imbuing it with power
passing it on as breath is passed
from one resuscitating another.

The word was meant
to be kept secret

and when he meditated
he would recite it
with the voice inside his mind

allowing himself to fall into it
become erased by it.

I googled Sanskrit words
that might bring about a
state of inner peace.

Ahimsa

Bhairav

Chaitra

Drishti

Esha

I could make
myself come

even if I didn't
feel like it

(to remind myself that I could)

and the thought
of the only time
my mother caught me
(half-hidden under covers)
made me smile

the smirk on her face

the moment suspended
in a funny breathless pause

and she'd said the most perfect
thing that a mother could've said:

"Are you doing magic?"

I tried doing magic

but ate a biscuit instead

then I walked to the window
and sat on the ledge
the dock outside, empty now.

The irony was that the ship
seemed to sway more
when it was anchored.

When the ship was in motion
the bow cut across the current
absorbed it
rode the crest of waves.

But the more it tried to remain static
the more the little waves disturbed
the hull with small irritating shunts.

I looked around the room.

It was small.

Opulent
compared to crew's quarters.

But next to an average
hotel room it was tiny.

I'd never been in first class
but I imagined the space there
was even smaller than the crew's
despite costing their yearly wage.

I picked up another biscuit

doorknob rattles

the sound trips
a small stone
into my belly

and for a heartbeat
I could again see
the tall figure
in the doorway

But it was only him

back from the gym

and when
he saw
the biscuit
in my hand
he said
the most perfect thing:

—Shall we get some lunch?

nine

> "Indeed, a quick perusal of the many excerpts describing the civilized tribes shows a uniformity in their descriptions of individual groups, and Filipinos in general: superstitious, lazy, ungrateful, distrustful, hospitable, submissive, imitative, musically inclined."
>
> —Benito Manalo Vergara, Displaying Filipinos: Photography and Colonialism in Early 20th Century Philippines

In the days leading up
to his first performance
we often went to the theatre
on the lowest floor
accessible to guests.

When it wasn't in use
he was allowed to practise
on the piano
that hibernated behind
a curtain at the far
corner of the stage.

The theatre was larger
on the inside
with seats curving around
a semicircular platform.

At the far end of the room
a small glass-walled booth
flashed red and green
turning the stage manager
into a Filipino Wizard of Oz.

I climbed down
to one of the middle rows
to give him feedback
on the quality of sound
from different points in the room.

His sound I knew.

But every hall had its own unique sound.
Each piano a different beast.

How hard was its action?
How bright its tone?
How will the audience
mediate its sound
with their bodies?

Over the years
travelling with him
to different halls and theatres
I grew to see
that it was a kind
of courtship

he'll approach it
so much larger than him

its colouring
like a poisonous frog
you shouldn't get near
let alone touch.

and they

would dance

he'll modify

the weight

of his fingers

cantilever

the load

of his body

coax sound

from the creature

bring it to song

and they

became

one

black wing

lifted high

gleaming organs

exposed

but as his fingers

became slippery

with sweat

I knew

that it was *his*

golden innards

laid bare.

ten

> "they say that in The Philippines there are three religions: basketball, boxing and beauty pageants"
>
> —@daughteroftheking

she lets me lick
the sweet glue
on the envelope's lip
and tells me
that convincing him (my father)
would be
the hardest part

she plays me songs
on a cassette tape
whose cover
has a drawing
of a hill on it
a little girl
some bears
a wolf in braces
pigs in houses
up the mound

—Which song do you like?

—I like, 'Be Brave, Little One'

she writes the lyrics
on a piece of fax paper

she sings a line *I copy like a lyre bird*

and we
practise
practise
practise

one day she brings home
a dress of blue tulle
that rubs my armpits raw

and then
she takes me
to the city

The theme song of 'Little Miss Philippines'
plays on the small black and white TV:

it's a small world after all
it's a small world after all
it's a small world after all
it's a small, small world

"my name is Loribelle Tuplano Spirovski
I'm five years old
I live in Santa Ana, Manila!

There is a saying:

In order to better my life
I must first admit what is wrong!

Thank you"

it's a small world after all
it's a small world after all

I win
the first round

the crowd
loud enough
to be inaudible

it's a small world after all
it's a small world after all

the next few weeks
passing in a blur of girls
in pannier hoops
the size of bassinets

it's a small world after all
it's a small world after all

and when I make it to finals

it's a small world after all
it's a small world after all

the last question
is something about
what I'd say to God
when I meet him in heaven (when I die, is what they mean)

and my answer is enough
to score the runner up sash

my mother's tears
like molten wax
my hair burning
under spotlights

the winner (the judge's niece from Zamboanga)
requires a translator
because she only speaks Spanish

her heavy flamenco dress
the red of rose petals
and blood

and
some time

after the pageant

the box arrives

on the back
of my uncle's bike

Styrofoam
still white
under holes
punched
into the lid

when they lifted it

something inside

alive

an infant macaque

tall as a collarbone
eyes like mirrors
ears like the
gaping mouths
of conch shells

they'd found it (my uncle went on)
among fallen
banana hearts
at my grandparents'

where it clung
to a ripening hand
abandoned/lost/
alone

so they'd brought her
to me
a *gift*
a token of pride

and I named her Tootsie
after candy that
I'd seen on TV
(though never eaten)

and Tootsie lived
in a cage for birds

wore a strap around
her ankle

rode the shoulders of uncles

crawled down their backs
to eager laughter

and sometimes Tootsie
sat in the cage

and watched
with glass eyes

I noticed
that if I looked
at her for too long

a pain grew

in my stomach

my limbs going heavy
as though
I'd been running

so I don't look

and played outside
with the other children
in the courtyard
between our houses

when Tootsie
tried to bite
my cousin
they kept her
in the cage
more often

and when it was
time to leave
we gave her
to a neighbour

who promised
to look after her (or so my mother tells me)

it's a small, small world

eleven

By the time I met him
my father went by 'Bob'.

A taxi driver (like De Niro)
for whom the road was
the last remaining equaliser.

He drove fast and often
which was how I learnt
that I could hurl the contents
of my stomach on roadsides
during long drives.

On the ship
the motion sickness
was constant.

Going outside helped a little
while the horizon could
trick my brain into thinking
I was on solid earth

—I'd breathe hard
smell the mineral ocean smell
lean far over the railing
until my hands disappeared
then the railing
then me.

But my insides felt like a toy
I once saw at a market in Manila:
a thimble-sized bottle half-
filled with red water
contained inside
a larger one
filled with blue.

If you tilted the bottle one way
the fluid inside the smaller one
moved in the opposite direction.

The little red sea inside my body
a counterpoint to the one
on which I travelled.

On the higher floors
where the waves
were less powerful
I'd drift from pool to cafe

reading in the Palm Court
or sitting in the trophy room
where plaques threw sunlight
in gashes on the walls.

Past the plaques
the mantlepiece had
a telescope and a globe on it.

Automatically I found
the familiar archipelago
(which to me always looked
like an old woman leaning
on a walking stick).

When I was a child
I'd wondered where I was
on the little drawing

the dot above the 'i'
in 'Manila'?

the hole inside the 'a'?

all smaller now.

Next to the globe
was a large conch shell.

I lifted it with both hands.

Heavy. Larger than
any of the shells I'd
ever found by the sea.

On either side of
the mouth's black hole
the lips were fleshy pink
fading to white
the ribbed skin extending
to barbs like a frozen explosion.

It was cool against my hot ear
and when I angled it firmly
against the hole the sound
was as clear as a word.

But the swell
of a wave made
the floor stutter

and the conch leapt
from my hand
into the air

tumbling
with a heavy rolling thud.

In the fall
a fragment chipped
skittered
across the floorboards.

I picked it up

placed it into my pocket
next to a book
the size of a baby's fist.

Beneath the book's
torn plastic case
I touched the cover's flap
and slid a finger under

stroking the pages
so oily from overuse
that they felt like vellum.

twelve

On Sunday mornings we went to
mass at Our Lady of The Abandoned
a Spanish colonial church built
by a tributary of the Pasig river.

From a distance it had the look
of stone, grey from a century of
exhaust, but touch it and watch
as it turns into porous adobe.

To get there we caught a *jipney*.
My mother impeccably made up,
her clothes old but well cared for
a pair of earrings framing her face
adding to the shine of her black hair
which was always kept short—

at the time I noticed none of this directly.

She always had a hanky bordered
with flowers folded neatly in her
handbag, inexpensive but precious.

And she always came prepared
with a folded *pamaypay* for when
it got too hot, or during the parts
of mass that didn't involve singing
when my attention would drift
and it would serve as entertainment.

The thin gold chain she wore (a gift from my father)
around her neck glinted against
her brown skin like a secret.

Because I was rib-height I hardly
remember looking at her directly
but always noticed her stride;
purposeful, with the straight-backed
elegance she perfected when she
worked as a lounge singer
in the time before she had me.

When she perspired, it wasn't
as I did, with sweat that pooled
in a watery moustache above my
upper lip. Her sweat was a dew
that nourished her complexion
heightened the colour of her eyes
and cheeks. And when she breathed
it was never harsh her shoulders
never slumped perfectly squared
even on the hottest days.

On church days, she was most beautiful.

The church of Santa Ana had large
metal gates and through it vendors
manned carts alive with garlands of
sampaguita flowers big as giant's teeth.
Another wagon sold rosaries of every size
and style; translucent candy-coloured ones
pious wooden ropes with crucifixes
large enough to impale a dragonfly
cords of delicate beaded glass that
winked in the sun and jewelled pieces

in slender glass cases relentlessly
guarded. Flowers masked the smell
of car fumes and waste and through
the church doors where the air was
thick with the smell of candlewax
all memory of the outside world
would be forgotten; and there
I would indulge in some selective
blindness, choosing to delay the
sight of the golden retablo at the far
wall, ferociously beautiful
unnerving in its glimmer and
spectacle. Instead we would turn
left, where row upon row of candles
melted in large metal troughs
beneath a statue of Christ, grotesquely
large, his fibreglass blood trickling
in a motionless cascade, his facial
expression flickering in the firelight.
His mother's statue was a few metres
away and smaller, waxen face frozen
in serene piety her open hands level
with my head, her bare feet surrounded
by plaster roses covered in hardened
candlewax. My own mother would
add to the mound, thrusting a candle
within the molten pool that she had
tipped her own melted wax into—
a fiery eye crying hot tears of worship.
Women and men neat and pretty
in the pews watched the spectacle
making pronouncements on neighbours
and family members, gossiping about
the young *dalaga* who'd blossomed
over the season. We'd find a gap to sit

catching one right at the front and sliding
across, my mother taking out her Spanish
pamaypay and fanning a breeze large enough
to reach me. And there, behind the priest's
altar, the golden retablo glowed
like the burning mouth of a cave, its breadth
divided into alcoves the size of human coffins.
In each niche, the porcelain countenance
of a saint: one clutches a book, the other
a staff, one is beardless almost boyish,
his neighbour withered grey. Stare for long
enough and occasionally a cleaner would appear
high up in one of the recesses, reaching
around to wipe an apostle's face, as if to rub
away tears. And when the priest's voice
begins to echo in the golden palace,
the people quiet, bow their heads,
inhale the incense and slow their fans,
making room inside themselves.
Time slows. I become somnambulant
resting on a padded footrest the colour
of oxblood looking up at the statue of the mother
elevated in the hierarchy of the retablo, my own
mother's head high above me her eyes
large her lashes like arrows pointing to the sky,
the man next to her staring,
his face a clenched fist.

> "That's God's country we're leaving behind, sure enough," said he, "and you'll find it out after a week or two in the Philippines."
>
> —Joseph Earle Stevens, Yesterdays in the Philippines

thirteen

—I'm starting a new book.
—Oh? What about?
—It's set in the early 19th century. A realist novel. One of the first great realist novels. If not the first.
—That sounds great. Can you read some to me before bed?
—Sure.

the sound of pages turning

—It feels like everything is a movie playing inside my mind.
—What do you mean?

—I don't know.

—Like I'm not real, or something. Like I'm trapped inside a cage.

laughs

—Ships can have that effect. It's probably just the seasickness.
—Maybe.
—And you're barely sleeping.
—I know.
—You probably shouldn't take too much Valium.
—I know.

—I miss our bed.
—Me too.

—This one's fine. But it's not the same.
—I know.

—How are you feeling?
—I'm ok. Just want to get the performances over and done with.
—I know.

—These people haven't changed since I was a boy.
—Really?
—Really.
—In what way?
—It's like…they never age. Like they've always been old. Always saying the same things to me.
—Like what?
—"I remember you when you were nine years old. You had more hair then."

laughs *laughs*

—I think being around the crew makes me feel insecure.
—What do you mean?
—I guess I'm not used to being waited on.

the sound of pages turning

—Or maybe it's because I'm not used to being around other Filipinos.
Memories and...things.
—What kind of memories?
—Oh, just things I've already told you.

the sound of pages turning

—I keep thinking about how tiny their cabins must be.
—Whose cabins?
—The crew.
—Right. Yes, theirs would definitely be smaller than ours.
—And how uncomfortable it would be for them on the lowest level.

—What do you think they do if they get seasick?
—I'm not sure.
—Do you think they only hire people who don't get seasick?
—Maybe. I imagine that's probably one of the conditions.
Or else they just have to live with it.

the sound of pages turning

—What was Ana-Maria like?
—My nanny? Great.

—Do you remember much from that time?
—Yeah, her voice. How nice she was on those early mornings,
practising before school.
—So strange that you had a Filipino nanny.
—And now I have a Filipino child bride.

laughs *laughs*

—Should we go to bed?
—Ok.

—Want me to read to you?
—Yes please.

—I miss home.
—Me too.

fourteen

—Gorgeous complexion!

she said eyeing my arms
with an appreciative smile
a battered crime novel clasped
in thin liver-spotted hands.

I smiled back.

—Thank you.
—What are you?
—Sorry?
—Where are you from?

and when no easy answer came
I asked her to guess
watching thoughts gather
under the roof of her mouth
shoulders squaring as she offered:

Brazilian?
Spanish?
Mexican?

and when I recited my own
two-sentence memoir
she "hmm'd" with bored delight
tuberose wafting from
her linen dress as she stepped
out of the ship's library.

The ship's library had the same sorts of
books you'd find at airports as well
as ones meant to simply fill space;
Encyclopaedia Britannica
heavy leather atlases
Lonely Planet travel guides

Some I'd read before

but when I picked one up
and skimmed the first page
it stared back blankly, a stranger.

Our own small crowded library at home
smelled of dust and cat dander
arranged according to a sequence
that only he could interpret
some plausibly intuitive structure
—almost musical.

I'd enter with a specific book in mind
hunting through shelves until my eyes
watered, determined not to ask for help
and be dragged to another book and then
another, adrift, pleasantly unmoored.

And I thought then
of the first book I'd ever received;
a birthday present from my father.

One of the kind popular in the nineties
personalised with your child's name.

It had been about a princess (me)
in a castle and some sort of
quest with a flying horse
(something to merit a plot)

but mostly I remember
seeing my own name in print

a concept rendered out of
symbols that lived in a book.

Between the pages
of one of the library books
I found a makeshift bookmark
on which the previous reader
had written a list of chores.

Clean garage for Clara
Dental appt
Cancel Steve
*98641****

I sat in one of the hard
leather couches for a while
with a book that I hadn't
understood on first reading

and by the time I reached
the second chapter enough
time had passed since my last
meal that I could allow myself
to walk back to the buffet.

"Got a jones for the smell of the place... tricycle exhaust and burnt coconut husks mixed into that warm wet air...morning rooster crows echoing and Jeepney horns and classic rock on karaoke...it all comes back to me when I daydream."

–@therealchristopherthomson

fifteen

before I met him
my father would send gifts
to mark each Christmas
and each birthday

a curriculum vitae
of care packages
full of books
dolls
hand-knitted dresses
from his aging
mother in Belgrade
and boxes
and boxes
of chocolate

for ages I believed that
my father was Santa
—an idea
that was reinforced
by the hideous song
'I Saw Mommy Kissing Santa Klaus'

and the fact that
my mother would
point at the sky
whenever she heard
a plane passing
telling me that
it was my father
"watching over us"

whenever a new box arrived
I would scour the surface
of every item
in search of traces of him

one year
he sent me a pair
of inline skates
which arrived in the heat
of the dry season
coated in the
melted remains
of Kinder Surprise eggs

—revolted
my mother
ran for a dishcloth
and while her back
was turned
I scraped my teeth
against the plastic
wheels until
my face was covered
in the sweet mess

he sent the picture book
the following year

but the package
that arrived
the year after
had perhaps
the most
profound effect

it contained a drawing
from his younger brother
an artist

a picture of me

a snarl of delicate pencil marks
that I carried with me everywhere
at breakfast
at the toilet
under my pillow
on the living-room floors of neighbours

until it became
sweat-stained
oily
like vellum

sixteen

whenever we'd visit
lolo and *lola's* house
I was allowed to borrow
one of the playthings
in the sitting room cabinet

knick-knacks that my mother
and her sisters had brought back
from Japan, Singapore, Malaysia

but what I always wanted
was the porcelain geisha
that my mother had received
as a gift from the Japanese
businessman she'd once dated

no one was allowed to touch it

the doll was suspended
in a half turn
tall as a small macaque
her red robe
embellished
with dancing dragons
wrought in golden thread
two miniature fans
perfectly articulated
in each hand
painted with a pattern
of bamboo leaves
her hair gathered

into the shape
of butterfly wings
lips painted red
eyes like commas

she came
with her own
delicate glass case

for nearly all
of my childhood
I thought it was
a model of her
(my mother)
and at night I fancied
that she moved around
completing the arc
of her dance
the hem
of her skirt
whispering
against the floor
of her cage

in the morning
I would check for any
change in her look

but she was always

as she was

years later

past midnight

unable to fall back asleep

I turned on the TV
and saw a grainy documentary
about a doll maker in Saitama

he wore traditional Japanese garb
and looked like film depictions
of samurai

one by one
he placed heads on a tray
(at first you couldn't tell they were heads)

painting each face
with a deftness
that seemed sped up

coiffed hair adhered to scalps
a painted widow's peak
to unify its face

their bodies were formed out of wire
and enclosed in padded cotton
upholstery like pincushions

heads affixed to each body
with tiny porcelain hands
pinned to the ends

they had no feet

instead torsos extended into a single
rigid form like a fishtail tacked
onto a weighted wooden base

when he dressed the bodies
in layers of silk
and embroidered fabric

the camera oscillated to his face
which had a look
of possession

he'd made hundreds of dolls
the camera panned to show
their miniature docile faces

similar but not quite the same
warped just enough
to be someone else

seventeen

performers got dressed
in a hidden vestibule
behind the theatre

to get there you walked
around the back of the stage
through
several
narrow
winding
corridors

and down
a set of stairs

once
not paying
enough attention
I tripped on the staircase
and rolled my ankle stumbling
onto the carpeted floor

so I learnt to reach my hand
around the interior wall and feel
for the light switch before entering

row upon row of sequined
jackets materialised before me
top hats and tulle skirts
bare-breasted mannequins
with their heads removed

the stumps of their metal
spines glinting dully under the
suspended fluorescent hum

there were handwritten
signs on office paper
taped to the metal racks
matching costumes
with shows and performers
and across the room
black, red, blonde and blue
wigs nested on the
mannequins' orphaned heads

it was almost enough
to distract from the nausea

until the next swell sobered
me to a higher elevation

once in the theatre
I'd sit in a middle row
while he practised the same
pieces I'd heard him play
on his piano at home
—that tamed pet
obscured under a pastiche of
fingermarks and breadcrumbs

I teased him about the colony
that was surely growing in the
wood beneath the ivory veneer

but never disturbed the film
of friendly dust that danced
with him when he played

I walked out of the theatre
and into the stale aircon
that floated on that windowless
level where a red velvet rope
cordoned off the lower floors

the crew's floors

I went closer
peering past the bend
in the staircase which crept
into darkness listening
for any sounds the crew made

edging
until I felt
the heavy rope
against my thigh

the longer I looked
the more the void
yawned open to me

until it filled
my entire field of vision

I opened my mouth

and let it enter

> "Having said all the above, towards the latter part of my career at sea I found a slow but steady erosion of the good old Filipino seamen values with more petty problems & minor violent incidents but they still remain the best & are value for the salary compared to the others."
>
> —cruisehive.com

eighteen

she was fourth of nine

skin sun-dark

rooster child

born feet-first in
typhoon-flooded rivers

volcanic dust staining
the whites of her eyes

when she was six
her sister took her
to a radio station
and entered her
in a singing competition

when she was fifteen
she started work
as a disc jockey
playing Freddie Aguilar
and 'Dahil sa Iyo'
on repeat teaching
herself to play guitar
on steel strings that bit
into the soft flesh
of her fingers

when she was twenty
she answered

the ad in the paper
asking her if she
"dreamt of travel?"
and "could sing?"
and became the first
in her family
to leave the country
sending wages back home
to *Papa* and *Mama*
while life played out
like the lyrics of a song

that was how she met
The Engineer

Bee Gees flares
soft brown hair
in a Hasselhoff tousle
lounging at the bar
with the rest of the
Енергопројект team

flanked by sisters she'd brought
over from the village
they noticed the foreigner
requesting 'Dahil sa Iyo'
and buying them cocktails
"like a real gentleman"

so after a while they made a pact

that whomever he should "choose"
would "go with him"

I stopped myself
before asking her
what she had wanted

and as for him
my father didn't hesitate
"It was always for her"

for a while he travelled

between his home in Belgrade
to wherever work sent him

and back to her

they courted like this

by the time my mother
was pregnant with me
they'd been living
with his family
in Belgrade for a year

his favourite story:
my stoic Macedonian
grandfather gives my mother
raw chilli dipped in salt
(as a kind of test)
and after she matches him
three for three
my grandfather proclaims
"This is my daughter!"

their best years
were spent travelling
across Europe in a rented
car hopping from one place
to another depending on
which countries allowed
Filipinos to hold visas

they married in 89

a small civil union at an office in Belgrade
only a few guests to mark the occasion

she wore:
an ivory skirt suit
padded shoulders
kitten heels
white tights
a bouquet
that trailed
ribbons down
her knees

but by the end of the year

protests at the Slovenian border
heralded the coming war

and theirs was the kind
of casualty rarely spoken of

she returned home so that
she would not be alone
when I was born

while he sought refuge
in a country so far away
it hadn't yet caught up
with its own history

—why couldn't we come with you to Australia?
—без визе. They say if a Filipino come, they never leave

I was born
in the autumn of 1990

a miniature of him

her daily reminder

my mother told me she chose my name
because she liked how it sounded

it shares ancestry
with 'Laura' and 'Lorelei'
originating from the laurel
or common bay leaf (*Laurus nobilis*)
native to the region close
to where my father was born

it means, 'victory'

nineteen

a splinter
of disembodied light

hangs
from the chain

—only a keychain
but in that moment

a completely foreign object

a bit of sun for a pet
(complete with its own leash)

when my cousin shifts the bag
shattered light tumbles out
in rainbows on the concrete

soon his father
will notice me watching
and follow my gaze
to the object

he'll put a finger
to his lips
and wink at me
as he creeps towards
his son's bag
slipping object

from chain
with a deftness
that appears sped up

the act only lasts a few seconds
but my heartbeat counts
in double time

and I don't look
when he palms me
the cold heavy object

I look only
when I am alone

and the object
in my palm
like water
made solid

a shard of
unmeltable ice

a frozen teardrop

heavy treasure

because I have
no pockets

I slip it
between waistband
and bare skin

cold enough
to make me shiver
cold enough
to nullify
the sun

the fabric sagging
with its weight
until it rests
against the hot
valley between
my legs

where I let it sit

until warmth
blossoms
somewhere
behind my navel

and it's the teardrop
I think about
when I lose
the gift my
mother gives me
for a birthday
present that year

as I hid behind
the sunglass-rotisserie
at the street market
and plucked another toy
(almost the same)
when the vendor's back
is turned

placing it where
the other one was

(I think my mother notices

but she doesn't say)

as payment

a snatcher walks past
my mother and grabs
the gold necklace
from her throat

leaving a gash
in exchange

and I learnt
how God
balanced
the weight
of things in
a celestial
game of give and take

on the day
of the snatching
my mother tells me a story
set in a cinema
years before I was born

she said that she
and her sisters
were only vaguely
interested in the movie
enjoying a reprieve from
the heat more than anything

when after a while
one of the younger sisters
noticed that a stranger's hand
was resting on her breast

and the anecdote seemed
to end there

the hand disembodied
from any real person

and I wondered
whether my aunt stayed
for the rest of the film

as though nothing
had been taken
from her

twenty

We'd been in bed
when it happened

pretending to sleep

the sun peeking
through a slit
in the curtains

the drone
of the ship's engines
a muted lulling
in the background
when the broadcast
blared from the speaker

echoing from everywhere
and nowhere

annoyed
he told me a story about
a Japanese cruise ship
he'd performed on
just before we met
where the captain
had aired daily
morning greetings
that woke all
the passengers

—Like a Soviet alarm clock. But everyone must've been used to it because no one complained.

and because he'd been
telling the story
we missed the beginning
of the captain's message
only catching
the part that said

"...waiting for news
but in the meantime
guests are encouraged
to wear protective face
coverings while outside
of their state rooms
until further information
is received.

"Wishing you all a pleasant day."

so we found

the paper bag

resting against

the cabin door

two

disposable

face masks

individually

wrapped

in plastic

blue

like the sky

on a clear day

he picked up

his phone

and I knew

he must've

been writing

to his doctor (his mother)

and after a pause

that seemed longer

because of the room's

quietness

he looked up

expression

illegible

blue eyes

sea-coloured

and told me

that

the world

had

changed.

PART 2

isa

in the beginning
there is
the sky
the sea
and the bird

tired of flying
the bird
asks the sea and the sky
to make islands
so it can have a place
to build a nest

they do

and the bird does its thing
and I guess it's happy for a while

one day
the bird lands on a rock
and pricks its foot
on something sharp

and the bird, enraged,
hits the sharp thing
hard enough
to split it in two

and the thing (a bamboo rod)
becomes more important
than anyone could guess

because on this island
bamboo are the children
of the earth and sky

so something amazing happens:

out of the fissure in the bamboo rod

two beings emerge

a man (*Malakas*)
a woman (*Maganda*)

the earth quakes
and calls on all
the birds and the fish
to figure out what to do
with the new ones

and it's decided
that the two should marry

they had many children

time goes by

and the children
behaving as most children do
aren't all that interested
in doing whatever
their parents were doing

and are punished
by their father
who beats them
with a stick

the children, frightened, flee

those who hide in rooms grow up to become island chiefs

those who hide in walls become slaves

those who hide in the fireplace become dark-skinned

and those who flee abroad have children of their own

and these children
in turn come back
to the land
of their forefathers

their skin
an entire generation
removed
from the sun
now white

dalawa

the ceiling of the airport
was so high it took
the balloon minutes
to touch it

crying all around
teddy bears held
tightly by the throat

there were so many
white people

I scanned the faces
of tourists for something
that looked like me

        I wanted him
        to stand out

                he didn't

"Is it him?"
my aunt asked

and I felt my
mother flinch
next to me

a shaking step
towards the crowd

edging a plank

and in a moment
of recognition

she detached
herself from us
and ran
swallowed
by the crowd

and she emerged
embracing one of the strangers

holding him in a way
I'd never seen her do before

and he was
made up
of every
male tourist;
large damp
ruddy skin
light brown
hair freckled
curling into
soft ringlets

when he came close
and tried
to embrace me
his odour
had the same quality
as mine did

after a long day
in the sun

he was shy
had the same
faraway look

at the time I didn't cry

stopped myself
from recoiling
each time he held me
emboldened
by my mother's display
of physical affection
with him

it took a while
to get used to
the bulk of him
at the table
in the bed
I shared with
my mother

who up to
that point
had been

mine

tatlo

In my first memory of the sea

I'm sheathed
in my mother's arms
like a dagger

the boat thrashes in the dark

a boy
hides
under his father's seat

wraps his arms
around thin metal legs

whenever the ship

leaps over a wave

his body levitates

my mother
slips a prayer book
inside the folds
of my clothes

only small
(the size of a baby's fist)

and shields me
from the storm
with the sleeve
of her shirt

hums a song in my ear

her wide eyes
black pearls
against a
darkening sky

apat

My aunt Gloria was already
waiting at the staircase.

Arms bent at elbows
feet splayed fists on hips
like a sugar bowl:
Matriarch's posture.

In my memory
she's an inverted tulip,
round, red, dressed in a ruby
kaftan that belled around her waist
tapering to small sandalled feet.

She had an oval-shaped face
black hair cut just below
the chin, a trench of grey
roots at the centre parting
the deep creases around
her drooping eyes arching
into colourless rainbows.

Her hands were so small
it was as though she wore
an armour of flesh meant to
give her frame more substance.

All the extended family came
for her firstborn's wedding
congregating at her opulent

mansyon after the ceremony
at Our Lady of The Abandoned.

We caught a *jipney* to get there
arriving sweaty and petrol scented
in front of the large metal gates
the children lined up and dusted in
baby powder before being allowed in
each child emerging sugar-coated
around neck and armpits where the
powder clung in patches like fungus.

The house was white marble inside
the entrance guarded by porcelain
vases large enough to hide a man.

The dark interior was cold.
I felt cold.
Something I'd never felt before.
I wrapped my arms around myself.

She took us on a tour of the place
so full of things I'd never seen
before, that our time spent inside
becomes warped in my memories
feeling like days instead of hours.

It was the first time I'd ever seen
a swimming pool so my mother
let me strip to my underwear
slide into the water and cling
onto the backs of older cousins.

The rest of the day was spent indoors
dripping smelling of pool chemicals wet

underwear balled up in my mother's bag
playing hide and seek in the dark.

In my dreams
I still wander those rooms
seeking out the cavern
of the home cinema
full of reclining leather couches.

Each already concealing a giggling child
who'd gotten there before me
their eyes shiny like cats in the dark.

One boy, unfamiliar with the concept
of hiding, simply huddled over the lap
of his seat like a large round pebble.

At some point we ran to the stone
balcony overhanging the enormous
backyard—beneath us a sea of people
tightly packed on the lawn.

It was then I experienced vertigo
for the first time, clinging to the
gourd-shaped concrete balusters
crawling backwards like a crumpled
table the floor hovering impossibly
over the crowd threatening to pull
me down over the railing.

(Somewhere in the back of my mind
I registered seeing a puff of white
that must have been the bride.)

I retreated into the darkness
and was drawn to the living room
which glowed a pale green light.

Inside, I saw that the light was
coming from a very large aquarium
and inside it, drifting, unseeing
was a small grey shark, slender
unreal, made of dream-fabric
the gaping slits of its gills
a repository for all things
that slipped into nonbeing.

I moved closer, inspecting its pebbly
cage, garlanded with transparent
green plants that bowed piously
whenever the shark passed by.

It never stopped moving.

Mouth hanging
dilating gills more alive
than its frozen eyes

much smaller
than what I imagined
sharks would be

small enough to have been a baby

and at the thought
tears spilled
down
my cheeks

until

a sound

from behind me

"Found you."

and I turned
to the dark figure
in the doorway
coming closer

coming closer

and then

AN EXPLOSION

don't breathe

silence

AND THEN ANOTHER

AND ANOTHER

from the
distant windows
a piercing light

ANOTHER

AND ANOTHER

trailed
by a
cackling
echo

fireworks

lima

The presence of surgical masks
in the days following the Captain's
announcement was by turns
reassuring and disconcerting and
then quickly and quietly ordinary.

People took swift silent bites of
their food suspicious of breaths
and the ambiguity of open mouths.

Whenever there were more
than four in a room guests would
fumble inside pockets pull masks
across mouths look into laps.

A few sought eyes surreptitiously
as though wondering
if they'd done something wrong.

Others dared judgement
their faces like clenched fists.

Some acted as though nothing
had happened, sitting at bars and
cafes, watching sport on TV screens.

It felt like all the lights had dimmed
or were suddenly too bright.

Empty now
we walked to the section
overlooking the Atrium
where stores sold men's
and women's clothing.

Headless mannequins
in last year's collections
manned by the same crew
who'd served us breakfast

Past the row of shops
there was a small gallery
displaying paintings,
prints and small sculptures
and across the gallery wall
studio photographs of
passengers celebrating
birthdays and anniversaries

The only thing of interest
was a ceramic vase the size
of a large cat decorated with
reliefs of yellow flowers
a large golden sunflower
at its centre, rows of seeds
and petals interlaced
in a withering tangle

For a class project in the second
or third grade we were given
a choice of seeds to grow
and I picked the 'Sunflower'
which I could read in English.

The diagram on the packet
was like the sun on the Philippine flag
its petals like sword-tipped rays of light

I brought it home
and my mother tipped
the dark little kernels
onto dry dirt

After a week
a thin periscope rose

twin leaves at the tip
like hands seeking alms
perfect

I'd touch their curious fragile vitality

but the plant didn't survive
and when I found
the green shoots shrivelled
felt it like a death

I wouldn't see
a real sunflower for years

until,
after hours
of monotonous driving with my father
carsick across the border of Queensland
and New South Wales
we came upon an immense field
of golden flowers

—What are they?
—сунцокрет

I rolled down the window
got to my knees head half
out and he slowed so
I could almost smell them

Large as human heads
some turned this way
others sunward, pious
each face distinct, familiar

I feared their near humanness

So never tried to plant
sunflowers again

Except when I married
I chose for my bouquet
a posy of sunflowers

their blazing faces
smiling knowingly
through the gauze
of my veil

"My husband and I have spent the last ten years cruising, and every time we see Joy it feels like we've come home."

—cruisehive.com

anim

A small brown fleck
floats a few millimetres
down from his left pupil
like a moon mid-orbit.

A second smaller speck
is mirrored in his right.

When he looks at you it's like
there are two sets of pupils;
a shadow-self peeking out.

> As a boy he met a gypsy
> who looked into his eyes
> and told him that he was
> destined for great things.

He turns to his side
and the globe of his iris is
a suspended drop of water
the pupil flattened into
an elliptical sinkhole in a
mossy bed of blue and grey
his lashes so fair they seem
almost transparent curling
upwards into the deep
shadowed hollows of his eyes.

I stroke the fair hair between
his brows to soften the crease
and his eyes close automatically.

He's naked, like always
and I wonder if he only
really feels like himself
when there are no
clothes to hide behind.

His milky skin roped with violet
and emerald veins so clear that when
he raises his arm exposing capillaries
I wonder how the skin contains him.

The hair in the hollow pit between
arm and rib is finely spun gold and from
the side with my face resting on his
shoulder, the length of his arm is a vast
beach, the freckles pinpricks of sand
a land of milky hills and purple valleys.

In one hand he holds a book by its spine
tendons tight against his skin, the way
it always gets when he's about to perform
his little finger extended like an antenna;
it's disproportionately long beside the rest
—a familial quirk and saving grace for a
pianist with small inflexible hands. (or so he tells me)

He gets up, breaking my wondering
and walks to the shower, absently
placing his book face down on the bed.

He's lost every bookmark I've ever
given him, so I tear my own in half
and insert it between the splayed pages.

Rolling to my side and sliding off the
bed to grab his bow tie from the suitcase
picking an undershirt and adding it to the pile.

I don't need to think about doing any of this.

For a while
I simply listen to the sounds he makes

and when he emerges at the doorway
a cloud of steam appears with him
making him look even more unreal.

He walks up to the clothes
not questioning how they got there
          braces
then puts them on, movements quick
practised, eyes glazed like a shark's.

And as the clothes envelop his body
one garment at a time he disappears

and I want to scream out his name.

pito

the sound of clothes rustling

—Don't make noise, ok.

(indistinct mumble)

more rustling

—No, not like that.

the sound of breathing

—Like this. Remember?

(indistinct)

the sound of fireworks

walo

Slip

through the crowd
and feel the fabric of
dresses against my legs

counting bandages
from melanoma extractions
on the heads of men
to distract myself
from the nausea

Benny Goodman rounds out
the sound of the audience
finding seats like homing
pigeons assisted by ushers
in black uniforms that
turn them into floating
heads against black walls

the aircon is turned up in
anticipation of the heat
that will build through
the sheer number of bodies.

For the performer   it will remain cold.

The stage lit with blue.

An aquarium.

Piano teeth bared white.

The woman sitting next to me
rests her walking stick against
the back of the seat in front
rings glittering as she looks
around with the open expression
of a child searching for her parents
fairy floss hair artfully wound
around a jewelled clasp wrought
into the shape of a dragonfly

    she's come alone

and I wonder if hers is one of the
gold-lettered names in the Atrium.

The permanent resident?
Old Rose searching for Jack
long dead.

And then the music stops
    and a staggered sigh ripples

the audience turning in unison
electrifying the stage with
their collective attention.

he steps out
into the blue

so much smaller than when he'd
laid against my chest an hour ago

far larger than anyone in the room.

He walks to the instrument.

Magnifies silence with his footsteps.

Sits a small distance from the keyboard.

And in the breathless pause before
he lays his hands on the keys,
I see it—
the thing that resides in him
laughs with his voice

leave his body

in its place an apparatus that
no longer seems to need air
the chest cavity opening like
a mouth as the first ringing notes
fill the spaces between our
bodies the sound coming
directly from his flayed ribs.

and the audience sways to the music
as though it belongs to them

after a few pieces he pauses
for remarks on the composer
for a tasteful joke

("They're Americans so best not to joke too much,
learned that the hard way")

but even as the tension in my
skull builds throat constricting
impulse to retch irresistible

the music echoes
in the chamber
of my chest
in swells that
seep through skin
budding into barbs
of sensation
down my arms

but then the dragonfly woman's
foot kicks out in the glitch of a paroxysm
foot connecting with walking stick clattering
to the floor hitting the metal part of the
platform with a clang that brings me back

the crowd bristles

annoyed look *annoyed look* *annoyed look*

he barely flinches

and when he finishes the final piece
and the crowd gives its tepid applause
I stand practically bounding from my
seat side-stepping the walking stick the
dragonfly and ten other passengers until
I reach the end of my row running for
the theatre doors which are opened
by an usher's floating head.

breathe

I walk to the stairs

lean against a handrail

the ship heaving

I climb

the sensation ebbing

as levels rise

until I am able to walk

unsupported

reaching the forked

road that leads

to the cabins

forgetting

for a moment

where I am

remove

shoes

dress

crawl inside t-shirt

lay sideways on the bed

he appears
five minutes later
wordlessly
removing
his own clothes

climbs
into bed

holds me

limbs thrumming

slowly unwinding

he pulls my shirt up
and presses his face
hard into the hollow
as though wanting to
break through bone
to search for himself

breathing so deeply that
I feel he'd been unable to
until that moment

feel the pulse in his head

neck muscles
hardened
into a bridge
down his spine

he places one foot
on top of mine so
our feet too embrace

body easing
against body

nerves uncoiling

he raises his head
and looks at me

through double pupils

> "The good thing about this job is the fair salary and im very much happy to serve the people on this ship any jobs thats suit my talent.
>
> The challenges are language barriers and ways of life and as im just an aspiring applicant i want to boost my talent/skills and to work with joy and pride."
>
> —cruisejobs.com

siyam

It rained
the night
we passed

Samoa

The Cook Islands

French Polynesia

but by daytime
the sun was
so bright
so hot
that all traces
of rain
had evaporated
from decks
from memory

pinpricks
of sweat
gathering
glittering
across my
bare thighs
the pool
rippling with
some invisible
stone skimmed

below the deck
passengers
who were unafraid
to leave the ship
(and others who feared
to stay aboard)
milled in ant-farm formations

I googled how long
ants could live
inside farms (2–4 weeks)

and what they did
with their dead (bury them)

thinking
of the enormous
ant and termite
mounds behind
the house
in San Jose
on the hill
where my mother
used to play
between shifts
at the family store

the *punso*
like inverted vessels
of reddish grey earth
smoothed into shape
by ant saliva
each one
tall enough
to bury a child

my grandmother
(not much taller
than a child)
taught me the words
to say when
we passed one

"Tabi tabi po"

and we took turns
making the strange
pronouncement
until the spell was cast
and we could
pass freely
from the *duwende*
that may have
dwelled there

we climbed
past the fallen
banana hearts
purplish red
like torn-up bits
of muscle
until we found
what we were
looking for:

a *gumamela* tree
redolent with
blossoms
large as hands

she'd pick a few
gut the petals
tuck them
under gnarled
fingers
crushing each
red tongue
in a plastic
bowl
until sap
perspired

and she'd take
a bit of wire
twist it
into a loop
dip the 'O'
into the liquid
lift it up
to my pursed lips
and tell me to blow

until the
glistening film

engorged

pushed out

like something
out of space

like something that
shouldn't be

sampu

sunlight
sunlight
sunlight

echoed

in waves

off the

tree-less

concrete

courtyard

making sweat pool
under my eyes
like stinging tears

I'm the first one out

but can hear my friend Jane

across the courtyard

screaming

at her mother's

screams

I slip back
into the house
to wait

walking past
my mother
walis tingting
in hand

sweeping
linoleum
vigorously
enough
to change
its colour
from grey
to white

the soles
of my feet
smearing black
the clean floor

"*Ano ka ba naman*, Lobel!"

and she raised an arm
to strike

afterwards
I wriggled
to the narrow

wooden shelf
where toys
were kept

grabbed them

walked to the settee

climbed up
and over
aluminium legs
and padded linoleum

and sat
back turned
to room

the dolls:
one in the blue frock
and another in a pink
gown that tore away
to a silver party dress
—my favourite
though the hair
had been brutalised
by cousin Ramon

I split the legs
into their full
ranges of motion
to see
the gaps
in the plastic

at the hinge
of thighs
where
sockets
interlock

once

I'd seen
the leg removed

pulled off
by a neighbour
in his doorway
a halo of light
rendering
his body
in shadow

and after

he did it

I'd stared

a long

time
at the gaping

hole

until
my mother
slotted it back
with a metal spoon

it made
a satisfying
thunk

later

I worked out

how to pull
the leg off
myself

labing isa

I met Jane when I came out to play
one day on the small communal court-
yard shared by our connecting houses.
She was giving the kids next door rides
in her father's wheelbarrow and when
she saw me asked if I wanted a turn.
I was shy so they called me, "*Makahiya*"
but she smiled anyway—"Come on!"
So I did. A bit scared. And she pushed
me in that dirty wheelbarrow soiling
the bottoms of my shorts, but letting
me forget my own shyness for a while.

Jane is a few grades higher than me and is
my best friend even though we go to class
in different parts of the school and I only
see her at assemblies when we gather on
the quad—even then, she has friends her
own age and would never go to where the
little kids sit (except that one time when
she came over to show me off to her friends
because I was the only white kid in school).

One day I'm walking over to her house.
Her mother is sitting on a plastic stool by
the front gate getting her nails done by the
lady who goes around the neighbourhood
doing nails for four pesos. Jane's mother is
round with an unhappy face but she wears
bright colours to hide it. Her father is out.
He doesn't need to work. He doesn't.

I walk inside their house through a narrow
hallway—there's a pedestal fan mounted in the
corner and the walls are the colour of puya flowers
and I see Jane sitting in the La-Z-Boy looking
tiny with her knees pressed against her chest.
She's watching a movie on the TV that her
father bought with her mother's inheritance.
It's *Titanic*. I know this because street sellers
had started appearing at every corner squatting
on *banigs* surrounded by t-shirts and bootleg
tapes of *Titanic* and other films with the same
actors as well as films about the sea like *Jaws*
and *Free Willy*. I walk into the living room
with the walls painted the colour of puya flowers
and it's like Jane doesn't even notice me.
Then I look around and I see that there's another
girl on the floor—a schoolmate of Jane's.
I watch them as they both look at the screen
with faces like statues: *Rose is entering the car.*
Jack holds out a hand to help her—except they're
not outside on a road, but in the part of the ship where
the bulky things that the guests have brought with them
are kept. He jumps in the front part where the driver
sits and asks her where she wants to go: "To the stars"
she says and pulls him through the window so they are
both sitting inside the carriage. And then the music goes
quiet so you can hear the sound of their clothes rustling
and their breathing becomes so much louder and for
a little while they just touch hands. But not like how
people usually touch hands; they hold their hands
up next to their faces so the fingers look like two people
pressed up against each other. Then he asks her if she's
nervous and it's him who looks nervous, and their eyes
are saying secret things to each other, so when she kisses
the tips of his fingers I look away from the screen

and turn to Jane, her limbs locked in the rigid
brace of her arms, her school friend frozen on
the floor clutching skinny ankles with Tipp-Ex nails.

She lets out a sigh (the friend)
and whispers something to herself.

–Anong sinabi mo?
–What?

–What did you say?

giggles

– I said, I'd let him rape me.

labing dalawa

I began to leave the
cabin only at night

while he slept

walking around
each deck listening
to sounds amplified
by collective sleep
become clear
as soliloquies

I stopped at the
sign of the arrow
(pointless now)
and moved in the
opposite direction
smelling the ship's
odours as I passed:
sterile aircon
kitchen fug
briny breeze

to my right
the sinking sun
left embers
on a velvet sea
and in the space
of a minute
the ocean
turned to pitch

and blinking
became one
with the night

I took the long way

walking around the
bow overlooking
the crew's deck
Astroturf plastic chairs
wooden picnic tables
—they'd have opted
for fake grass to make
it easier to clean

under one of the chairs
a piece of litter gloats

after a little while
a young man walked
towards the railing
absently tapping
his cigarette
on the butt of its box

he leaned
over the barrier
hip jutting out
in contrapposto
like the statue of David
black hair netted
brown skin dark

against his uniform
smoke
ascending
from his lips
in a
slanted
pirouette

On the highest deck
I entered the Palm Court

saturated in moonlight
that flooded through
slanted pink windows

colourless now
as everything in the room

my footsteps
on the wave-patterned carpet
were so quiet

and I paused
at the edge of the
wooden dancefloor

preserving
the silence

larger
than I remembered
the laminate floor
was made to look
like a sun
or a whirlpool

a dozen rays of light
and dark-coloured wood
extending in a languid coil
fusing in a circle at its centre

in the dark the circle
looked more like an orb
raised optically from the floor

so that a large black mass
appeared to sit perfectly
at the heart of the spiral

I squinted
not sure whether
I was imagining it

but as I took
a step forward
it was (really) there

a rounded mound
of raised wood

like a smooth
pregnant belly

budding from the floor

and logic

fell

then

dread

I could not bear
to break
eye contact

so slid forward

until I was feet from it

closer now
it looked more
like a polished pebble

the size of a person
huddled over

and the longer I looked
the more details
came to me

the shape was longer
than I first thought

with deep grooves
carved from the sides

so that it really did look
like a person
folded over its own lap

child's pose

and as the thought came

the mound

twitched

slightly

so slightly
you'd be forgiven
in thinking it
a trick of light

but after
a minute

it was standing

shorter than me

(the size of a child)

shadow-coloured

stiller than any living thing

and the nausea
was a solid thing
in my chest

as though
the onyx child
standing before me
had its twin
inside
my ribcage

bile
burned

and I swallowed
the scream
as the thing

again
            moved

reaching an arm
upwards

as if in greeting

but
the arm
descended

seemed

to grasp

for the space

between its legs

  its torso
    bending
      forwards
       in the grotesque
      parody
     of a bow

the hand

entering

and when

the hand

emerged

it was held up
to me

like an offering

and the thing
it held

caught
a fragment
of moonlight

which
slithered
through the
cut glass

and threw
shards
of rainbow
coloured light
all over
the dance
floor

I bent over and purged

labing tatlo

the
waves
collide
with one
another
collide
with one
another
crests
crashing
into troughs
ripples
coming
in endless
swells of
order
of chaos
of endless
trembling
trembling
trembling
stare
long
enough
and
pat-
terns
echo
in
motion's
aftereffect

after
after
after
after

after
after
after
after
afterwards
afterwards
afterwards
they asked me about it
it

"Where did he touch you?"

and when we finished
I got to go
and play outside
outside
outside
outside
outside
outside
outside
outside on

on

the tree-less concrete
radiant with
sunlight

PART 3

—Do I seem distracted to you?
—Sometimes.
—Often?
—Not often.
—How often?
—Only sometimes.

—Does it feel like I'm not with you?
—No.

—What is it like?
—Like you've got a lot on your mind.

—'Cause I don't want it to be like it was before.
—It won't be.

један

because of our proximity
to each other on the ship
because of our proximity
to each other on the ship
because of our proximity
to each other on the ship
because of our proximity
to each other on the ship
because of our proximity
to each other on the ship
because of our proximity
to each other on the ship
because of our proximity
to each other on the ship
our habits and daily routi
nes were more noticeable
because of our proximity
to each other on the ship
we would often come
across the same person or
couple or groups of people
doing the same things
at the same time every
day because of our prox
imity to each other on
the ship people were more
~~paranoid~~ mindful of how
close we all stood to each
other because of our prox
imity to each other on the
ship we could see each

other's eye-colours above
the blue surgical masks
because of our proximity to
each other on the ship we
could see each other's fear.

два

—God, I wish I was still smoking.

laughs *laughs*

—Probably good that you aren't.
—I guess so.
—They're saying it's worse for smokers, you know.
—I guess so.

—What do you think it will be like when we get back?
—I'm not sure.

—Do you think everything will be different?
—Maybe.
—What does your mum think?
—That they'll be scrambling to put a vaccine together.
—Your dad?

shrugs

—He reckons all travel will stop for a while.

—Maybe we should get off the ship.
—What? Now?

—No, not right now.

laughs

—Ok.

she takes the bookmark out

and begins to tear the edge

—I'm finding it really hard.
—Finding what hard?

continuing down one side

—(*whispers*) Keeping it together.
—What did you say?

—Being on this ship for so long.

and then the next side

and the next

and the next

—Maybe you've got a monkey on your back.

she reaches the centre of the bookmark
—What?
—A monkey on your back. Something that's troubling you.

the bookmark is a thin coil of paper

—Ok.
—Ok what?
—Let's get off at the next port.
—What?
—I'll tell them we don't feel safe on the ship.

the sound of hands touching

—A few passengers have already disembarked.

—Will our parents be ok?

—I don't know.

три

before he was a taxi driver
he was an engineer

and before that
he was a smoker

and before that
it was the war

and before that
he divorced his second wife

and before that
his first son was born

and before that
his first daughter died

and before that
his name was Slobodan
and he was a gardener

Echinocactus
crowned in tiny florets
berry-coloured Barbary figs
—plants that came
with their own armour

carnivorous *Stapelia grandiflora*
and fuzzy *Cephalocereus senilis*

with hairlike spines he'd taught
me to stroke like rabbit's fur

he'd inherited a mass of *Portulacaria*
from the house's previous tenant
whose fleshy leaves I'd pick
break in half and drag across
the concrete footpath making graffiti
that evaporated in the sun

often a stray thorn would embed itself
in the tough skin of his hand
and I'd have to extract it with the kissing
tips of a pair of tweezers
the barb so translucent I could almost
see through it to the wound
in which it entered him

if the thorn was stuck deep
he showed me how to prise
the skin apart with a needle
dragging the lighter's spark wheel
against his thumb until the needle's
tip became briefly incandescent
bruise-coloured, purified

I'd slide the skin apart creating
a new wound—intensive labour
lasting minutes, feeling like years

and once open the splinter would rise
just enough for the tweezers
to embrace it

the first time he asked me
to remove a thorn
he'd lifted his hand (just a little)
as though afraid of burdening me
with its weight
his palm
heavy
thick
work-roughened
the intaglio of fingerprints
deep enough for him to sit
in its troughs undisturbed

I burrowed the needle
until warm blood rose
to fill the lines of his skin
like a red river
and I'd feel him surrender
the full weight of his hand
in mine
full
of the burden
of him

> "The hardest aspect about working on the ships is the time away from family. Sometimes you don't see them for nearly one year. There's not much you can do, except be strong and pray."
>
> —maritimejournal.com

четири

in Yugoslavia
my grandparents had lived in
an apartment close to the city

but during the warm
spring and summer months
they stayed on an island
off the Dalmatian Coast
in a house fashioned within
the remnants of an old castle
built before the Ottoman Empire
had come and gone

in my late teens when
I'd sheepishly tried to ingratiate
myself into my father's world
I watched a documentary
on the Ottoman occupation
of the place that would become
Yugoslavia until it was again unmade
in the last decade of the 20th century
—a riot of grisly impalements
and gory fatalism that still
revisited anxious dreams

on the island
they'd owned twelve
small plots of land
cultivated into vineyards
of grapes from Macedonian
hills harvested for wine

that would see them
through the long winter

after my grandfather died
and the plots were sold off
two were left
to the eldest grandchild

my father's first son

a boy of sixteen
when the war broke out

he'd followed his mother's family
over the newly created border
between Serbia and Croatia

and then over
a few more borders
much harder to cross

my mother
taught me of these things
from letters they'd exchanged
over nine years

pages and postcards
and scented valentines
through which I memorised
the swooping curves
of my father's penmanship

her letters in turn
were written on paper so thin
it crackled like a small tin roof

her tidy bighearted handwriting
making deep indents
so I could almost read
the words like braille

her hand pressing
into the sheet
hard enough
to pierce
through time

through space

to touch him again

> "During the decade after World War II, the name Slobodan (means 'freedom') became the most popular Serbian male name, and it remained so until 1980."
>
> —wikipedia.com

пет

the hot earth shrugged against
a sky the colour of wet linen

steam ascending from scorched
concrete eager to become rain

grandchildren scattered like
windless kites in the courtyard

while neighbouring kids waved
from behind their mothers' legs

—friends whose faces I'd only
see again on posts about weddings
and the children they'd have

I don't remember seeing Jane

my grandmother's fingers skimmed
the rivers that flowed from her milky
eyes; not to staunch, merely to wet

to revel

then she put her arms around me
her face committing to memory
my mother's face, our pilgrim
hands reaching for the shrine of her

the last memories

stray dogs barking
an elegy of dripping wax
the crackle of rosary beads

how I used to cry when my mother sang

to understand what happened
you first had to leave

and again
I was dreaming
though wide awake

and from behind
one of the neighbour's
doors the tall shadow
stood watching me
for the last time

шест

we'd used almost
everything I packed—
each object carefully chosen
for the comfort of future selves
as though they were our children

what books should we bring?
will I feel like writing?
will I want to wear this?

and with the packing done the cabin at last
had lost some of the sickening intimacy it
accumulated over the time we'd spent there

then I showered one last time, studying
the long strands of hair I'd plastered on the
white tiles to stop them clogging the drain

the rest of the day was spent revisiting
all the places that had been our favourites
and then all the places we hadn't thought
to go: casinos cinemas billiards room
the room where people played cards

and by evening we sat at the lounge
in front of the large indoor waterfall
flanked by twin bronze seahorses

—Any song requests from the audience?

"Dahil sa Iyo" my voice said

and before I could change my mind
the lounge singer winked, keyboardist
entering with the first echoing notes

Dahil sa 'yo nais kong mabuhay
Dahil sa'yo hanggang mamatay
Dapat mong tantuin, wala ng ibang giliw
Puso ko'y tanungin, ikaw at ikaw rin

Because of you, there's a joy in living.
Because of you, life is heavenly.
I never lived before, never felt a single thrill before,
My heart stood still before, Darlin' I'm in ecstasy.

by the time we were back in the cabin
I was tired enough to not need a pill

the wave of sleep coming
as instantly as being put under

an echo of the only time
I'd ever been anaesthetised

the pregnancy

stopped before it could become more
than a few instances of morning sickness

(my body trembled
only slightly
in the paper gown
before the rush of
cool surrender swept
up from rib-height

melting through
my sternum
creeping behind
collarbones
and the flesh
around my throat

the nurse's face
swimming
as if in a dream)

and in that place
without colour
without sound

the fingers
on its tiny hand
warm with the heat
of a thousand
dying stars

closed around
my forefinger
like a leaf

like a dance
of a thousand hands
in miniature

седам

in the dream
I am inside the walls

the space
between
beams
so narrow
my body
has to
shrink
to fit

what light there is strains
through pinpricks in the drywall
and again I feel
the poking in my belly

when I look
the dark thing protrudes from my navel

like a finger growing, growing until the stamen emerges fully

the petals unfurling
like butterfly wings

I am in the bathroom

the tiles scrubbed
so clean that grout
is worn away leaving
gaps for the worms
to crawl through

—my uncle walks in
with a jar of salt to
pour into the cracks

a dark thing
emerging

unravelling

from the hole

in no time

I am on the bridge

a low-slung barrier
over the Pasig river

concrete balustrades
covered in traffic soot

blocking out segments
of oily river water

if I sit low enough
I could miss it entirely

catching only its smell
which passed through
the pane-less windows
where plastic flaps are
rolled into cigarillos

it was possible to hold
your breath for the
length of the bridge

but in the last quarter
electric stars swam
at the edges of vision
and there was no choice
but to sip the sulfidic air
and catch a glimpse
of the pyramids
bordering the edges
of the polluted pool

rafts of floating detritus
scattered across it
and once a man
(a boy)
young and slender
punting from
one ziggurat
to another
with a long
bamboo rod
floating on tyres
bound to boards

that came from
the riverside

I watch him
from behind
my mother's arm
my feet clinging
like a monkey's
to the metal legs
—clinging tighter
when the *jipney* leaps
over potholes

he sinks
the rod until
it's walking-stick height
and I place a hand
inside my pocket
to stroke the oily paper

the painted sky colourless

but as he leans
over the raft
to gather more

I am him

and I let go
of the bamboo rod

gliding

into the river

my body carried
by undertow
by waste

only the sound
of the steel excavator
waiting

beyond pillars of refuse

stamping
stamping
stamping

"The Pasig River used to be an important transport route and source of water for Spanish Manila. Due to negligence and industrial development, the river suffered a rapid decline in the second half of the 20th century and was declared biologically dead in 1990."

—wikipedia.com

осам

—You don't remember me,

the man said
as he came up
to where we stood
in the queue

his tone
of someone
midway through
a conversation

—but I came to your Mozart at the Opera House
when you were five.

—I was nine.

—No, I'm certain you were five.

glances at his head

—You had more hair then.

laughs *laughs*

and satisfied
the man turned back
to his wheelchair-bound wife

—Jesus, how long is this going to take?
—Not much longer now.

and it really wasn't that much
longer before we reached
the head of the line

the young woman at the desk (Adriana, Romania)
shooting swift glances at our faces
checking them against the miniatures
inside our passports her green eyes
shrill above the blue surgical mask

I wanted to tell her that it was definitely
me—sure that I no longer resembled
the photograph in the tiny booklet

but she handed back both documents
without preamble and we walked
to the metal detectors for the last time
our suitcases wheeled by the same crew
who'd attended to them when we first
boarded our footsteps clanging against
the metal railing attached to the pier

everything normal

except for the masks
blue as the peaks
of icebergs

beneath my feet
the pier swayed
with some invisible wave
my own mask
clinging with each
ardent breath
the sky a different
sort of blue
than I remembered

I see friends
shaking hands
saying "How do you do?"
They're really saying
I love you

I thought of the little two-
bedroom apartment we moved to
when we arrived in Australia

a tree-lined street
full of paperbarks that wore
their own skins like flayed cloaks
rows of eucalypts with red resin clinging
to pale torsos like wounded Christs
each tree *alive*—the way people were alive

the tart berries of Lilly Pillies
were so pink they looked poisonous
—a wind landed on the crown of
one making the leaves shudder

and from a weathered branch
a magpie sang its broken glass song

unfastening me from the old life

in solidarity with the new one
my father planted a seed
in my mother
as though to say all had been
~~forgiven~~ forgotten
all made anew

девет

there were animals in the next place

cats mostly

but also dogs

unbred
teats hanging

—I'm worried they don't feed them here.

they don't
I wanted to tell him
they're all going to die
and felt the words
foaming at my mouth

—They'll be fine.

he walked to his third stray

borderless, roaming, some
skittish, most reaching back
for the hand that reached
for the soft fur behind their
ears—both hungry for
the other's consolation

I sketched him with fingers
greasy with chip oil

the ship's inertia lingering

we were guided up a hill by
a trickle of bodies that took
us to narrower lanes and
wider ones, moving slowly
up the cobblestones fringed
with stores selling every kind
of bag, shoe, scarf, next to
restaurants overlooking mounds
of sweets in rainbow clusters

two stray cats shepherded us
to a fountain, where seagulls
(far larger than any I'd ever seen)
uprooted the dormant air
making fallen leaves dance

it was at the fountain
in the middle of that large square
where all things seemed to meet

time flattened
under paving stones;
the temple a ruin-marked
spectacle whose spiked
minarets and burnished domes
pointed skywards—as though
to show a direction in which to follow

  we stepped barefoot over the threshold

cold stone under our feet worn concave
by worshippers by emperors by slaves
the boundless nave adorned by holy gazes
only half-concealed by veils eliding history

and when the whirling air
was punctured by the call
to prayer, like an eternal
flower blooming and wilting
in endless waves, marking
everything it touched, its spectre
made my bones sing, passing
beneath the archway where
faded Byzantine dolphins
stewarded the passage
of pilgrims, of time;
a palimpsest of gods

we exited the square with the stream
of bodies, up another hill and down
some other winding lane where an
ancient graveyard rose out of the earth

behind the headstones
kittens stalked tiny lizards

down and up until we came upon
a mildewed gateway older than the stones
and moss underfoot, and through it,
a room of men tossing pebbles
into shallow black wooden boxes

we took a table and I, the only woman,
waited for protest, but were silently

served tea instead, in delicate tulip-shaped
glasses rimmed with gold—I lifted it
by its lip revealing the single sugar-cube
                                        beneath; a gift

the men wore knitted hats and beanies
the heads of the eldest capped by black-
tasselled fezzes the colour of faded blood
each table padded with velvety fabric the
texture of a child's skin, a smoothness
every now and then interrupted
by the dark spectre of a cigarette burn,
the men's chatter a carpet of sound
that I sank into, surrendering
to its foreignness, the abstraction
of its music accompanied by the rhythmic
clacking of the boxes and the stones
the men were throwing—around us
a young boy with long lashes circulated
his jacquard jumper halfway zipped
a heavy-metal shirt peeking between
the folds, camel-eyes scouting for a
craggy finger raised or a brow arched
in his direction—he strides with a brass
tea-service and pours liquid amber from
a height, the steam billowing onto the face
of a kitten who watches the room imperiously
                              all of them are my father

on our last morning, we rose early enough
to catch breakfast on the upper terrace
the sprawling sunlit centrepiece of food
blinding me to anything else in the room;

crisp cucumbers, wedges of tomato, fat
little cigars of rice wrapped in dark vine
leaves glistening with oil, eggs halved
and laid end to end like rows of startled
eyes and twenty different types of cheese

it was impossible to try everything

—I wish I was as hungry as you in the mornings.

he nursed a coffee cup the size of a baby's
fist, while his scrolling left hand paused

—They're calling it a pandemic now.

there was music playing from somewhere
on the terrace—a song from the fifties
that brought to mind European streets
and balmy Mediterranean summers

I looked at his double pupils and watched
them quiver, my hand gently stealing
to his forearm, stroking absently

I turned to face the room—actually looked
at it—and was dazed by the expanse of
light raking across the surface of the world

though it was a terrace, it was wrapped
in glass, tall and wide enough to offer a
perfect picture of the landscape; roofs and
windowpanes of shingled houses frozen
in the act of climbing on top of each other

and further back, gold-leafed domes
that absorbed sunlight like the leaves
of an enormous vine—and there again
those colossal seagulls (or were they albatrosses?)
billowing onto rises of pale weathered stone

and the sunlit world seemed to stretch on
the longer I looked, details flickering in
and out of clarity; on a distant balcony
a woman wearing a headscarf was hanging
a long white sheet, a child beneath her
pulling at the cloth from between gourd-
shaped balusters while on the horizon
a long cabled bridge coupled opposing shores

and there, across the entire left side of the
terrace, the full breadth of the wide river;
a boundless stretch of crepe-paper, gathering
mass, seeming to defy the gravity of the earth
challenging the very corpus of the sky
cut off by the line of the terrace ceiling

an implausible world

supple

the way that it used to be
when we were children

I touched the streams
that flowed down my face
not staunching, merely wetting

revelling

десет

he arrived too early

on the other shore

more distant

in that funny see-
through box

than when he'd been
living inside her—her warmth
channelling his warmth

as he scissor-kicked
and flung himself
at the world
at our voices
at her

he arrived with skin
the colour of bruised figs

wet creosote hair spiking
to a point above
his fontanelle
like a monkey

but the holes in
his box were
large enough

for our arms to
fit through

our expressions hidden
by blue paper masks
that made us strangers
even to ourselves

while he—my brother
completed his
strange
transparent
exile

my mother said that
he'd arrived
ahead of time
because he couldn't
wait to see us
any longer

the exit wound
through which
he entered (the world)
a wan smile
sewn into the
underside
of her abdomen

she said that
in his rush to get here
he hadn't quite
"finished"

and had to
wait in the box

until enough of him
had grown
to face
the world

in her paper gown
my mother sagged
with serene
exhaustion thinking
perhaps
of everything
she'd done everything
she'd survived
to get to this place
to get to him

she'd allowed
me to see
only some
of what it had
                    cost

but I remembered
the longing
in the eyes of
men who'd
watched her

while the rust
of her own loneliness
crept into the black
pearls of her eyes

my father held
his fourth child
with the look
of a gardener
accustomed
to planting things

and whether he'd
thought then
of his other children
or whether
the pain had
become a thorn
so deeply
stuck
inside of him
that he no longer
recognised
the sting
nothing
but a passing shadow
across his deeply
lined face
hinted
at what he felt

when it was my turn
to put an arm
into the box

my brother's fingers
clung to me
belonging there

tulip mouth seeking
pomegranate skin
unbearably soft

        and it was like
        first touch
        again

        so warm it erased
        what preceded it;
        burns
        cuts
        the scaly touch of
        fingers so abrasive
        my skin came away
        like silver on
        a scratch card

I smiled
at her—at my mother
as she celebrated
her birthday

her first
of the new millennium

a whole future ahead

and in a few days
it would be
my tenth
birthday

Glossary

Abaca: [*Musa textilis*] a species of banana native to the Philippines, also known as Manila hemp. Its durable fibre is a versatile material notably used in garments such as the traditional Barong Tagalog.

'**Ano ka ba naman?**' in Tagalog this phrase means, 'What's wrong with you?' but the literal translation is, 'What are you?'

Bangus: [*Chanos chanos*] milkfish. National fish of the Philippines.

Bani: [*Milletia pinnata*] a fast-growing, leguminous tree with a wide crown of drooping branches.

Banig: [noun] A mattress, carpet or mat, especially a mat made of woven palm fronds.

без визе: [Serbian] Bez vize, '"No visa'."

Dahil sa Iyo: a song written in 1938 by Mike Velarde Jr, for the movie *Bituing Marikit*. It became a hit in the United States.

Dalaga: [noun] a young woman who has passed puberty but is not yet married; an eligible young woman.

Dinuguan: a savoury Filipino stew made of pork meat and offal, simmered in a rich gravy of pork blood, chilli, vinegar and garlic. Variations of the recipe occur in different regions across the Philippines.

Duwende: a creature from Philippine folklore. They are small humanoids that live in mounds of soil, anthills or termite mounds. If not shown proper courtesy, they are said to cause illness and suffering.

Енергопројект: [Serbian] Energoprojekt is a Serbian construction company with headquarters in Belgrade, Serbia. Founded in 1951.

Gumamela: [*Hibiscus*] a large flowering shrub native to warm, temperate and subtropical regions throughout the world.

Jipney: [noun] a hybrid type of bus made from WWII Jeeps abandoned in the Philippines after the war. Since the 1960s, Jeepneys have become a cultural symbol for the Philippines, and are known for their brightly decorated exteriors with paintings of popular and religious themes.

Libag: [noun] grime; the dirt that accumulates on skin.

Lola: [noun] grandmother.

Lolo: [noun] grandfather.

Maganda: [adjective] beautiful, attractive, enticing, lovely, charming, pleasant.

Manghihilot: a folk healer found in many provinces of the Philippines. 'Hilots' often incorporate massage and other traditional methods of identifying energy imbalances in the body.

Malakas: [adjective] strong, powerful, potent, mighty, influential, loud, athletic.

Manay: [Bicol Central] respectful term of address or honorific for a young woman or any woman older than oneself.

Nipa: a house on stilts indigenous to the Philippines. Designed for the Philippine climate, it is raised from the ground to prevent flooding.

Pamaypay: a type of traditional handheld fan from the Philippines.

сунцокрет: [Serbian] Suncokret. Sunflower.

Tabi tabi po: [expression] in Tagalog this means 'Excuse me' or 'May I pass?' These words are addressed to the spirits that live in the trees, grass or forests.

Tatay: [noun] father. Derived from the Spanish 'Tata'.

Tinapa: a Filipino term for preparing fish or meat by smoking.

Tita: [noun] derived from the Spanish 'Tia'. A term for the sister of either parent. An affectionate or honorific term for a woman of an older generation than oneself.

Tito: [noun] derived from the Spanish "Tio". A term for the brother of either parent. An affectionate or honorific term for a man of an older generation than oneself.

Traysikel: [noun] tricycle; motorcycle with a sidecar for passengers.

Tsinelas: [noun] derived from the Spanish 'chinelas', meaning 'slippers'. Originally made from abaca fibre.

Walis tingting: a type of broom made from the centre-rib of a Buri palm leaf. Commonly used in the Philippines.

References

It's a Small World is a song from 1963 by Richard M. Sherman and Robert B. Sherman.

What a wonderful World is a song from 1967 by Bob Thiele and George David Weiss.

Dahil Sa Iyo is a song from 1938 by Mike Velarde Jr. My description of the song is taken from taintwhatyoudo.com/category/personal

"Tita" and "Tito" definitions in the glossary are from en.m.wiktionary.org/wiki/tito

The Tabi Tabi Po definition in the glossary is from idsemergencymanagement.com/2019/11/14/what-are-the-pamahiin-in-the-philippines

The glossary entry for Енергопројект is sourced from db0nus869y26v.cloudfront.net/en/Energoprojekt_holding

Acknowledgements

To Terri-ann, I can never thank you enough for giving me the chance to tell this lonely little girl's story.

To Simon, Mireille, Felicity, Andrea and Milica, the first readers of this book, thank you for your love and generosity. This work would not exist without the time and energy you shared with me.

To my mother, thank you for your unending love. I would not have made it this far without you.

To my brother, thank you for saving me, exactly when I needed.

To my father, thank you for always trusting that I knew what I was doing. I love you more than I can say.

To Simon again; my home, my world, my everything.

About Upswell

Upswell Publishing was established in 2021 by Terri-ann White as a not-for-profit press. A perceived gap in the market for distinctive literary works in fiction, poetry and narrative non-fiction was the motivation. In her years as a bookseller, writer and then publisher, Terri-ann has maintained a watch on literary books and the way they insinuate themselves into a cultural space and are then located within our literary and cultural inheritance. She is interested in making books to last: books with the potential to still be noticed, and noted, after decades and thus be ripe to influence new literary histories.

About this typeface

Book designer Becky Chilcott chose Foundry Origin not only as a strong, carefully considered, and dependable typeface, but also to honour her late friend and mentor, type designer Freda Sack, who oversaw the project. Designed by Freda's long-standing colleague, Stuart de Rozario, much like Upswell Publishing, Foundry Origin was created out of the desire to say something new.